THE UGLY SILENT TRUTH

VINAYAK TANDON

ISBN 979-888591407-9

THIS ANTHOLOGY IS DEDICATED TO ALL THE AMAZING WRITERS WHO CONTRIBUTED WITH THEIR EXEMPLARY WRITEUPS.

Contents

Acknowledgements

WE THE EDITORS OF THIS BOOK WOULD LIKE TO EXPRESS OUR SPECIAL GRATITUDE TO ALL THE AMAZING WRITERS WHO TOOK PART IN THIS ANTHOLOGY AND WE ACKNOWLEDGE THE WRITEUPS FROM ALL THE AUTHORS:-

VINAYAK TANDON, ANSHIKA TANDON, SYED FAYIQ AHMED, SHUBHANGI YADAV, KASHISH ARORA, PRANJAL JAIN, ALINA HUSSAIN, SUNPRRET KAUR, RISHANSHI SHARMA, HARSH MALHOTRA, SAMARTH SINGH, PREETHIKA PARTHIBAN, RADHIKA RAWAT, STELLA DIMITROVA ,GAURI KAPOOR .

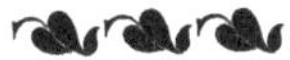

Foreword

- **SO IT IS HERE. "THE UGLY SILENT TRUTH."**

FOR SO LONG I HAVE BEEN PLANNING FOR THIS AND THIS IS FINALLY HERE. FIRST OF ALL I WOULD LIKE TO DEDICATE THIS BOOK TO OUR PARENTS (ASHISH & NIMMI TANDON) AND MY SISTER(ANSHIKA), WHO HAVE BEEN MY BACKBONE THROUGH OUT THIS JOURNEY. SECONDLY I WOULD LIKE TO DEDICATE THIS BOOK TO MY LOVELY WRITERS. WITHOUT THEM THIS BOOK WOULD HAVE NEVER BEEN COMPLETE. AT LAST ,I WOULD LIKE TO THANK THE ALMIGHTY FOR HIS ETERNAL LOVE AND SUPPORT.

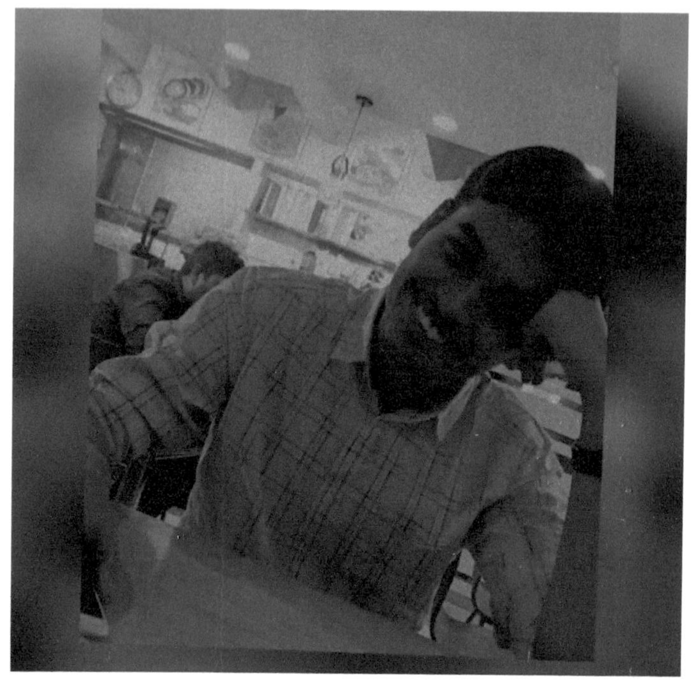

VINAYAK TANDON(EDITOR AND COMPILER)

ABOUT :-

THE EDITOR AND COMPILER OF THIS BOOK IS VINAYAK TANDON. VINAYAK IS A GUY FILLED WITH JOYFULLNESS, ENTHUSIASM AND AN URGE TO ALWAYS LEARN AND IMPROVE HIMSELF. HE IS CURRENTLY STUDYING IN CLASS 10TH AND HAS BEEN AN ARDENT READER AND

WRITER. HIS PASSION FOR WRITING HAS BEEN THERE FOR A VERY LONG TIME AND THE PASSION TO IMPROVE HIS CRAFT HAS AND WILL ALWAYS BE INSIDE HIM.

Preface

THIS ANTHOLOGY CONTAINS WRITEUPS OF EXTREMELY TALENTED AND UPCOMING WRITERS. THIS ANTHOLOGY TAKES YOU THROUGH THE HARSH REALITY OF TODAY‘S SOCIETY AND MAKES YOU FEEL EVERY WORD OF EVERY CHAPTER THAT IT CONTAINS.

I PROUDLY WELCOME YOU ALL TO WITNESS THIS AMAZING EXPERIENCE. I WELCOME YOU ALL IN "THE UGLY SILENT TRUTH".

CHAPTER ONE

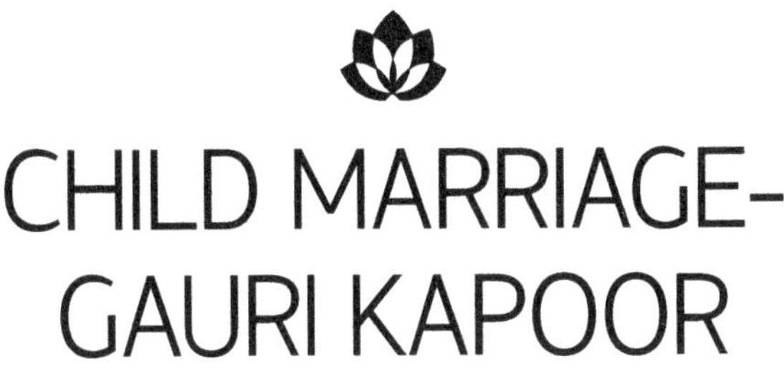

CHILD MARRIAGE- GAURI KAPOOR

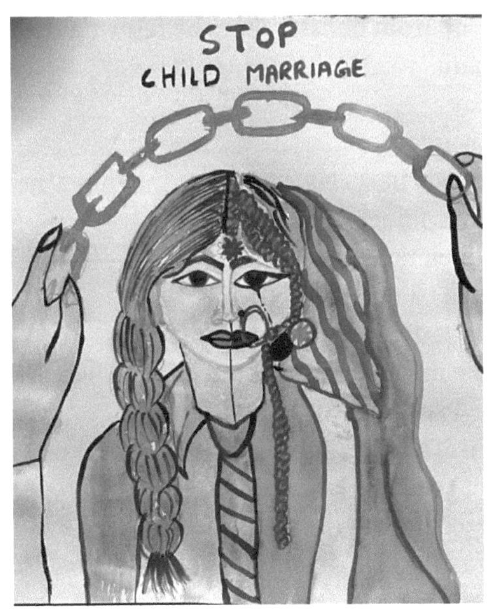

CHAPTER TWO

That Day -Vinayak Tandon

PREFACE: This poem is about a girl who was heinously raped by three men and was left to die. but she was somehow rescued and escorted to the healthcare. when she woke up from her slumber she felt what has been put in this poem.

That day
I could never forget
My life Turned in such a way
I could never forget

Three men raped me
Well it wasn't a rape
My lifeless body was left at their mercy
What made it worse was that one of them was Daddy

I begged and begged
They did it. They did it
I cried and cried
They just did it

They ran through my body
They left me with scars
They left my body
With stabs and marks

Time heals every wound
Sure it would
I am not sure
That this would
That day
I could never forget
My life turned in such a way
I could never forget

CHAPTER THREE

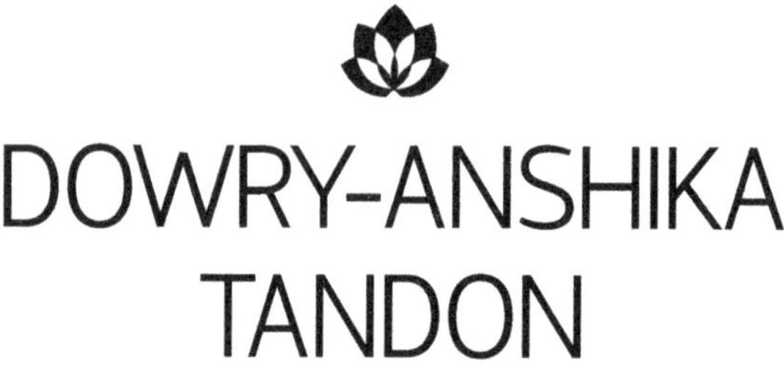

DOWRY-ANSHIKA TANDON

BIO:- THE WRITER OF THIS STORY IS ANSHIKA TANDON. ANSHIKA IS A GIRL FILLED WITH JOYFULLNESS, ENTHUSIASM AND AN URGE TO ALWAYS LEARN AND IMPROVE HERSELF. SHE IS CURRENTLY STUDYING IN COLLEGE AND HAS BEEN AN ARDENT READER AND WRITER.

"I don't want to marry him, paa ." Yeah this was what I said to him when I came to know that my father paid INR 10 Lakhs , as dowry. My dowry. Before I further more into the story let me tell you all about myself. I am kritika, a software developer in Bangalore. The man that I was supposed to marry would be earning less than me. But the only thing that "hampered" my marriage was my physical looks. I am not as good looking as society wants a girl. "Fair, slim". And I am pollar opposite to it. But that didn't hinder me becoming what I am. But from the part of the society that I come says that every girl should get married. Now they fixed my marriage with this guy, a tall , fair guy yeah a pretty enough guy for a girl like me. I felt that guy was a good person because he never made me felt what the people around me did. The day of the marriage came. Everything was going good when just before the 7 vows of marriage something stopped the parents and the guy himself, from the marriage . The parents of the guy secretly discussed something with my father and when the talk became a bit serious, I intervened. I asked them what happened? While my father was asking me to keep quite, that guy told me that my father had not paid the complete dowry money. That was the moment when I lost my mind. Why should I give money to someone else to marry me.And that was the first time where I stood for myself. I outright rejected the marriage. And that was probably the best thing that I ever did.

CHAPTER FOUR

POEMS-PRANJAL JAIN

Bio: Pranjal Jain is a first year student at Daulat Ram College, DU currently pursuing Economics honours.She likes to try new things.She is a cheerful and an open minded person whose hobbies are Writing and Dancing.She is a social service volunteer at NSS of her college.Shc has bcen the academic scholar of her school for consecutive five years. Her hometown is New Delhi and she lives in a nuclear family.

First poem: FLAMES OF FIRE

LShe has wings ,she knows how to lit But still she is asked to fit

She is a powerful soul

But still she gets a foul play

She is a butterfly,with wings made of fire She can fly and reach the pinnacle and Wherever she wants.

II.She is a queen ,she is a diva

She can dress as she wants

She is a hero,why only a heroine

She can play her male counterparts And can set the stage on fire ,the stage of life

III.She is a winner, give her a fair chance to try Something new, Something unique Something she wants to do

She listened to the roar of thunderstorm She fell in love with the fragrance
In petrichor
She searched the night sky for shooting stars She has an unvoiced yearn to explore
V.Then why is she hiding away bruises with words
that would touch her slowly fragging soul.
It's the time to voice those unvoiced whims
And stand up for the cause
For World should be a place to appreciate talent
And not to putoff one gender.
V.She has wings,she knows how to lit them with fire.
SECOND :Disregard if a girl is born
Disregard if she tells her own wishes,
Disregard if she tells what she wants to wear,
Disregard if she wants to educate herself
And live the life of her dream,
Disregard if she takes her own decisions,
Disregard if she does whatsoever she likes,
Disregard in whatsoever she thinks is good for her.
II.She is herself a disregard
Now it's a high time she
Opens up her mind and
Change those pretentious smiles to natural ones
And live the life of her choice

CHAPTER FIVE

A Hundred Pansies-SHUBHANGI YADAV

BIO: Miss Yadav, currently in her junior year of high school is a freelance writer from Delhi. She has produced a handful of poems and stories in the recent years and engaged in a bunch of co-curricular contests. Fond of books, Miss Yadav keeps herself occupied with novels and stories from around the world. The young aspirant hopes to excel in her field of interests and emerge as a youth speaker in near future.

STORY:

Afonso Library, an old library near the Church of Cross Miracles in Goa used to be my favourite place to hang out. I've decided to give it another visit today. I walk upstairs looking at the gate of the library, it's still an old wicket gate of the walnut wood. I remember coming here the last time. It was the month of December and the coldest December of my life. I went in without thinking which book I wanted to read and a voice falls on my ears, "Souls like you barely visit the library these days but you are always welcomed here." It's Miss Ledger, the librarian who has been working here for years now. I remember how she would always hug me after looking at my scar on the neck but never asked how I got it as if she already knew it. After she hugged me that day, I went to the corner in the library where all the lonely women got lost. The corner had dirty shelves but those dirty shelves trapped the ugliest truths of our society that were covered in lies, that's what Miss Ledger used to say. I would always hear those shelves calling my name but my heart was impaired after the death of my beloved so I would avoid taking risks of seeing those shelves.

I was in the corner but not near the dirty shelves. While walking away from them, I found a paper lying on the floor and picked it up. The paper I picked had a drawing of a book on it. The book was named, "A hundred Pansies" and near the drawing, there were four numbers "12,21,49,99".

Out of nowhere the light bulb over my head, it dropped.

I screamed and the paper fell from my hand. I breathed deep and slow so my hypotension doesn't kick in. There was silence. No one heard me screaming but in me, I had chaos in my veins as I heard something from the dirty shelves in the dark. I wanted to run away at that time but I knew, my curiosity would turn into a poison if I ran away from the undiscovered. I tightened my fists and started walking to the shelves. Trust me, they had the ugliest books of all time. Books so old, torn and absurdly arranged around an unpleasant odour, that I got to know why even the people with the worst taste didn't seem interested in these books. But my subconscious mind was acting strange. It made me pick up the book and when I read the title of the book, I dropped my jaw. The book was named "A hundred Pansies". Few seconds ago, I was holding the drawing of this book on a paper but now I am holding the actual book. Since when did coincidences become so scary?

The author's name wasn't mentioned on the book cover so I looked inside and read what was on the first page:

For my lovely liars

I turned the next page, it was empty.

I kept turning and found writings in different languages till I reached page number 12. 12 was also one of the four numbers I found under the drawing of this book.

I started reading.

Pansy 052 here,

Sorry I lied. It was me who stole my parents' jewellery worth 10000 dollars but if I didn't then I'd be dragged down to the stairs by my husband and they would lock me up in the basement just like Maya for not fulfilling the dowry desires of my in-laws. I wish people were more human.

I know I sinned but I don't seek forgiveness, I seek death.

I was feeling a little upset after reading this but maybe this is just how the author wrote the story.

I kept turning and found stories in other languages until I turned to page 21 which was also another number mentioned below that drawing. I wonder if someone knew I only understood English and wrote the page numbers with English stories below the drawing.

Anyways reading page number 21.

Pansy 079 here,

Sorry I lied. It was me who aborted Ruhani's child but I couldn't see her being violently harassed by her family for carrying a girl child in her womb. I didn't have a choice.

I know I sinned but I don't seek forgiveness, I seek death.

Even though I couldn't find a proof of the story being real or fictional but they were really heart breaking and I noticed something, both the stories ended with the same line "I seek death".

I quickly turned to the third number mentioned below the drawing, page number 49.

Pansy 093 here,

Sorry I lied. It was me who threw acid at the face of my sister's husband but I was more fed up than anyone else in this world. He often abused my sister for not having a fair skin and asking for money from her every month just to cover her "considered ugly" face. My sister would call me every week and cry. Me and sister tolerated enough, so I decided to throw acid on her husband's face without telling anyone and now his face was also "considered ugly" one like he thought about my sister. He deserved it.

I know I sinned but I don't seek forgiveness, I seek death.

I have no idea who wrote these stories and all of them ended with the same sentence. After reading all three stories about dowry, I suddenly remembered what Miss Ledger said, "Those dirty shelves trapped the ugliest truths of our society covered in lies."

I took a deep breath and turned to the fourth and the last number, page number 99.

Pansy 099 here,

Sorry I lied but I had to kill my brother Madhu becaus-

....

I dropped the book.

Madhu. That's the name of my late husband who got murdered and her sister-in-law was kidnapped and murdered too.

I didn't want to read further or think about this anymore but these stories of dowry, death, abuse, abortion.... they all seem true.

Tears sliding down my cheeks as the old memories flash Infront of my eyes. What wrong could my husband do to be mentioned in this book of ugly truths?

I pulled courage up my guts and decided to read further to find out.

Pansy 099 here,

Sorry I lied but I had to kill my brother Madhu because I was protecting someone and he was too inhuman to be alive. The scar on the neck of his wife wasn't because of the glass frame accidentally falling on her when she was sleeping but because of my brother intentionally dropping the glass frame on her neck. I saw it and confronted him. The glass didn't do much damage to her. Meanwhile my brother took me to another room and told me that he wanted more money from his wife's family as he was unsatisfied with all the luxury he got as dowry in his wedding. Even after receiving so much, he wanted more but when he couldn't get it, his wife became a burden for him. He told mc all about it, thinking I would help him out killing his wife but I developed a strong hatred towards him for this. It's shameful that people like him exist in this world. I told him that I would inform the police so he said, "You will if you stay alive. "And then he proceeded to kill me with the piece of glass he had in his hand. I defended myself, the glass was really near my neck but I pushed it towards my brother's chest and it pierced his heart.

Madhu died.

I know I sinned but I don't seek forgiveness, I seek death.

My hypotension kicked in.

Everyone thought that the murderers of Madhu kidnapped his sister because she caught them killing his brother and hung her up by a tree but now, I know the truth.

It was a suicide and all the people who wrote these stories, suicided afterwards.

That explains why all of them end with "I seek death."

My hypotension created scarce of blood in my head and I fell on the ground. My throat was dead, I couldn't even say a single word or call someone. I was dying.

The wind blew through the window and I looked back at the book as the pages started to turn. A page from the book flew to me and it said, "Only ugly books can show the ugly truths behind the silent dcaths of pansies (women) who were covered in the dust of lies, hidden in the shelves no one wanted to visit."

This was the last thing that flashed Infront of my eyes before my soul left my body. I died that day.

It has been 15 years since that December and Miss Ledger still works here.

She finds me staring at the corner where I died, the corner where the lonely women and their souls got lost just like mine.

She burns the book "A hundred Pansies" and whispers in my ear, "Souls like you barely visit the library these days but now they will never."

CHAPTER SIX

CASTE:PRIVILEGE OVER WORK- SUNPREET KAUR

BIO: Delacruz is an intriguing person, with a very curious mind and who loves to wander the wonders of the world. She has a deep interest in giving contribution for the removal of social evils from the society.

Acknowledge from the type of work,Geeta tells to behold,Blood is the not the right to curse,Shudra and his born.Sanatan dharma, the path of life,The first n foremost,A beautiful means but cuz of vice,Made a judgy brawl.Scheduled caste are still untouch,Met like dirt n drawn,Following then unfollowing much,A new trend to dawn.Made of sand, of vein and thrush,How different at all?No caste no creed, laws to crush,Only human to call.

CHAPTER SEVEN

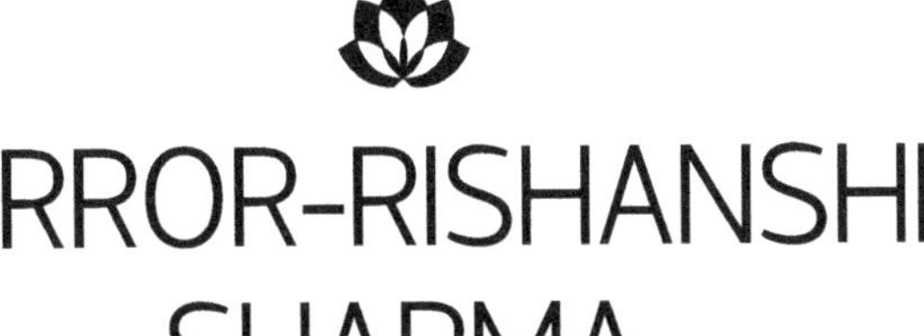

MIRROR-RISHANSHI SHARMA

BIO:

With sparking eyes and beautiful smile looking in the mirror, she dreamed a dream that she longed for .A dream which will give her a profound happiness, that'll make her eyes shine with gratefulness.An illusion she will carry in her big eyes as she faces the reality with a smile.As she lives in a world that contradicts with the world she wished for .this world speaks the language of money not humanity.Living in the bars of patriarchy, miles away from parity

CHAPTER EIGHT

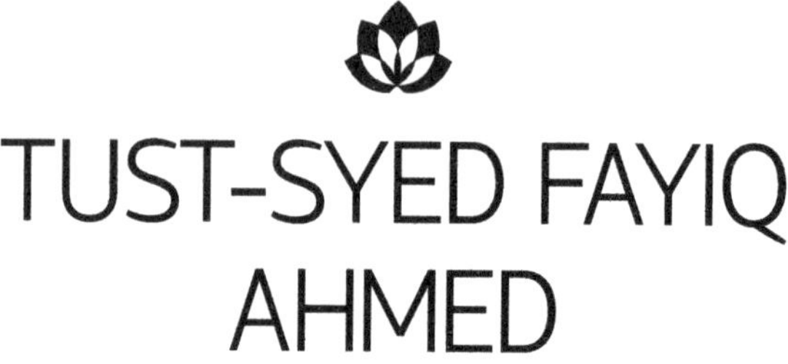

TUST-SYED FAYIQ AHMED

BIO: Hello reader! I hope you liked the previous chapters of this book. The chapter that you are going to read ahead is written by aspiring write Mr. SYED FAYIQ AHMED. The author is an engineering student who lives in Karnataka, India. Fayiq's hobbies are to write poetries in Hindi {shayeries}, write stories for different anthologies and read books. He has a shayeri account in Instagram named as @adure.alfaz where there are many shayeries and song reels. Fayiq is wanderlust, quick learner and a friendly person.

POEM:

A beautiful twilight reminds me of, my childhood. A girl needs a selfless mother in her life, who indicates her to take the right part of her life situations which she had to face. In 1980, when I started my school I was a non - studios child up to primary.

My father was a feminist and my mother was always against me, which made my father respect fill out in me but loved my mother till today and ahead. In front of my eyes my brother was loved more than me, which made me discover about gender inequality, I was not allowed to move out frequently and was not guided about the world, which made e anti-social and sinless to believe in people.

I was the only girl child from my family's generations to entre in higher secondary studies. Over that time my father quoted me that "Higher secondary changes life, so maintain good friends and good character the rest of the time".

In 1992, when I wished to join an degree course I was scared by negative people that being away from my parents would distract me from my studies. Through much negativity I continued my studies by distance education. When I was 19 years old I got married.

I completed my degree with many obstacles after my marriage. After marriage, I got my eyes open towards the world and faced many difficulties in being in a stereotypical big- joint family. My husband was working in abroad, so the family member seeing alone treated like a maid and my husband as a money bank which lead to no saving for personal use.

In 1998, I got my first child after 5 years of my marriage but didn't had any family member around me as my husband was back from abroad and we were not financially stabled. I did not knew how to grow up and take care of new born small babies, so it took me a lot of strain to take care of my first child.

Then after 2 years, I got my second child which lead to increases in financial downfall of my family. After seeing the conditions for long three years, in 2003, I continued my higher studies along with taking care of my family. I was antisocial person use to get nervous to talk to any of strangers. By god's grace, my husband again flew to abroad in a year.

I completed my double degree by 2005 along with success over antisocial and got appreciated by all college staff members for completing projects on time and completing degree after even having two children.

In 2006, my husband toke us along with him to abroad. I faced strains to get adjusted to new environment. My double degree was turned beneficial towards my children's study. My husband used to do shift-job so I quitted my job idea to take care of my children's. I didn't want to make my children's antisocial and nervous around people so made them to get mingled with everyone.

By the grave of almighty, my kids studied well, participated in every events of school and respected everyone. We made few properties back in our home country and made ourselves financially stabled. We enjoyed a lot over there until 2012 in 2012 where unfortunately we had to leave the country my elder son passed his 10th when wc lcft the country.

To make my child study higher secondary we took advises from close ones but everyone gave wrong advises and wished for families downfall. My child completed his higher secondary within two years and then for degree we decided not to take advises from any chameleons so me, my husband and my child discussed and toke decisions.

In 2018, my first child got competed his degree and second child was in degree. Now my first child is in job and took almost of responsibilities of me and my husband.

Back to the present twilight of 2021, I am happy and thankful to almighty to make my family get successes after long years of struggle. I am happy both of my children have settled in their life.

Well, this was an amazing life story of women whom I know closely. That's true that when you struggle by yourself you get an amazing success. It was a lovely journey with you reader, hope to see you again in this journey of life.

Here I go with a small ending poetry.
In 21st century women are driving out,
But still few are not allowed moving out.
Those pretty faces are smiling,
But still few are crying.
They are making friends in the world,
But still few are scared of strangers in the world.
Being happy is a wonderful choice,
But still few don't have that choice.
It's common for them to go on a night out,
But still few don't know what night out is.
Those have choices to get married,
But still few are force to get married.

CHAPTER NINE

Patriarchy-Curse To Society: KASHISH ARORA

BIO: Kashish Arora, is a 18 year old girl lives in the capital of India Delhi. She is very ambitious and hardworking girl and pursuing her carrer in Law in DME college. Her hobbies is reading books and sketching on her free time.

Patriarchy- The word itself describe so many things. The system which put all powers and give authorities to male member of the society, which is not the right decision for betterment of society. Patriarchy is the main reason of gender discrimination. It's not only about women but it's about creating misbalance among nature. Patriarchy is not only about giving powers to male members but not giving rights to women.As we all know about the landmark judgment of supreme court regarding the rights of daughter on there parents property. But the judgments cannot blur the reality of society and this judgment will take a long time to accept people because our patriarchal thinking entrenched in the roots of our society so badly that it is very tough to take it out. The reason for lack of education, female foeticides, maternal rapes etc... is the patriarchal society because this give the authority and rights to the male members of the society.Patriarchy is the obstacle of women life. It is very easy to say and very common phrase that women now have all rights and they are competing with men but nobody really see the obstruction she is facing regarding her journey. Before marriage she need to ask her parents for further studies and after marriage her husband and in-laws. The path is definitely not easy and it's answer is same "THE PATRIARCHAL SOCIETY".Women don't have there own house is so common phrase. They either have there parental home or in'laws home or his sons home but not there own but why? Whenever property is distributed it is said that husband belonging is now yours but they can't have the small piece of land by her name. The ans still remains he same "THE PATRIARCHAL SOCIETY".People say time changed but still the obstruction in women life remains same does'nt matter if she is getting education or not but she is always answerable to her parents , in-laws , husband and society.Patriarchy is not only a restriction for the social but it's a curse and it's root is so huge that a judgment for daughters property is not enough to remove it from the society. People must change there mentality towards the society and must consider everyone a human being rather then judging anyone on the bases of there gender.

CHAPTER TEN

DOMESTIC VIOLENCE ACT, 2005 - SAMARTH SINGH

INTRODUCTION:-

Are women safe at home with their partners? Where we see women standing side by side with men and even doing better than them in every field but at the same point, we get to see women are being raped, abused, tortured in their own home by spouses or partners. An estimate published by WHO indicates that globally about 1 in 3 (30%) of women worldwide have been subjected to either physical or sexual intimate partner violence or non-partner sexual in their lifetime. Domestic violence is deeply rooted in India. The National Crime Records Bureau (NCRB) 2019 reports that the majority (30.9%) of all the 4.05 lakh cases under Section 498A of the Indian Penal Code (IPC). Under this section there comes an act called THE PROTECTION OF WOMEN AGAINST DOMESTIC VIOLENCE ACT, 2005. It is an act by the Parliament of India made to protect women from domestic violence. It was brought into force on 26 Oct 2006 by the Indian Government and Ministry of Women and Child Development. It deals with both marital and non-marital (live–in) relationship as well

What is domestic violence?

Definition under the act says that any kind of violence committed by someone within the aggrieved person's domestic circle is called domestic violence. It can be done by their partners and ex partners, immediate family members, other relatives, and family friends.

It includes physical abuse, as well as mental and threats to do the same, here are some specific definition for these

PHYSICAL ABUSE

Physical abuse is the most common form of violence. It is an act that causes body pain, harm, or danger to life, limb, or health or impairs the health or development of an aggrieved person. However injury is doesn't need to be a major one. For example, your abuser slaps you few times causing only minor injuries that don't require you to visit a hospital. Although the injury is minor but the slapping would be considered as domestic violence.

VERBAL AND EMOTIONAL ABUSE

You may not think you are being abused if you are not being hurt physically. But emotional and verbal abuse can have short-term or long term effects that are as hard as physical violence. It involves the destruction of the victim's self-worth, insults, and attempts to scare you or control you, including those with regard to the inability to have a male child.

SEXUAL ABUSE

Sexual violence is the most common form of domestic violence. It includes not only sexual assault and rape but also harassment such as unwanted sexual touching, incest (sexual intercourse or sexual intrusion between family members), pornography. It's also known as molestation and the offender is referred to as a molester or a sexual abuser.

ECONOMIC ABUSE

Economical abuse can be of any kind, such as a husband preventing his wife from pursuing her carrier or a job outside the home, preventing her to study further, take her pay, causing damage to her property. It also includes the alienation of assets whether movable or immovable.

How to file a complaint against domestic violence

1. LOCAL POLICE STATION.

1. Victim can directly reach their local police station and file a case against their abuser under Section 498A of IPC.

2. SERVICE PROVIDER: SECTION 10

2. Registered non-governmental organizations (NGOs) fall under this category. They can help and encourage victims to file the case. They know the right procedure to move forwards in such cases. SNEHA

Foundation, Urja Trust Foundation, Maitri Foundation, Hothur Foundation are some of the NGOs you can contact.

3. MAJISTRATE: SECTION 12

3. Victims can directly reach their Judicial Magistrate of first-class or the Metropolitan Magistrate, within the local limits of which:-

- Victims can complain where they reside.
- Can complain where abuser resides.
- Can complain where violence happened.

The magistrate shall fix the first hearing of the case within three days of the complaint and the Magistrate shall Endeavour to dispose of every application made under sub-section (1) within the period of sixty days from the first hearing, but usually, it takes more time.

4. PROTECTION OFFICER: SECTION 8 & 9

4. Protection officer is appointed by The State Government in each district for women's safety. Protection

officer shall help the Magistrate in the execution of his duties under this act by reporting to the Magistrate about domestic violence incident in such form and such manner as prescribed, upon receipt of an allegation of domestic violence and transmit copies thereof to the police officer in charge of the police station within the local limits of whose jurisdiction domestic violence is claimed to happen. He must ensure that legal assistance is provided to the aggrieved person under the Legal Service Authorities Act, 1987. He must maintain a list of all service providers providing legal help, shelter, and medical facilities in a local area within the Magistrate jurisdiction. He must provide a safe shelter home if the aggrieved person requires and provide a copy to the police station and the Magistrate having jurisdiction in the region where the shelter home is located. He must examine the victim medically if she has physically suffered and forward a copy of the medical report to the police station and the Magistrate having the jurisdiction where domestic violence is alleged to have been taken place. He must ensure that the order of monetary relief under section 20 is followed with and executed according to the procedure prescribed under the Code of Criminal Procedure 1973. The Officer shall be under the superintendence of Magistrate and shall perform duties levied on by the Magistrate and the Government by, or under, this act.

Features:-

Victim resources

Under the act, the victim should be provided with proper medication, shelter, counselling as well as legal assistance whenever needed. **Counselling: Section 14** At any stage of proceedings under this act, the Magistrate may direct an aggrieved person to undergo counselling with any member of the service provider who holds such qualification and experience in counselling. **Proceedings to be held on camera: Section 16**The Magistrate may conduct a hearing on camera if either party desires to protect their privacy or in case of any medical emergency. # **Rhea Laila Pillai v. Leander Adrian Paes.** In this case, the court noted that cross-examination was of a "personal nature" and parts of proceedings were held on camera. **Residence order: Section 19** Protection or restraining order is an order used by the court to protect a person, alienation on assets, or to restrain the respondent to remove him from the shared household # **SR Barta v. Smt. Taruna Batra** In this case, the court held that under section 17(1) of the act wife can claim a right to live in the shared household which means house belonging to or taken on rent by husband or house which belongs to the joint family of which the husband is the member. **Monetary relief: Section 20** The respondent is supposed to provide relief to meet the loss incurred, including loss earning, medical expenses, loss caused due to the destruction, removal or damage to the property, and for the maintenance of the victim and her child. Custody orders: Section 21The magistrate at any stage of hearing can grant custody of child or children to the victim, with visiting rights to the respondent but the Magistrate can restrain rights if he found respondent visit harmful to children.

Conclusion:-

Domestic abuse evolves as society changes in fact it emerges in a new form as it happened during covid - 19 lockdown. The Indian government has taken many steps against it such as Section 498A, Section 304B, and The Dowry Prohibition Act 1961, and the Protection of Women from Domestic Violence Act 2005, and the Prohibition of

Child Marriage Act 2006, and Schemes like 181 helpline number, One Stop Centre, etc. However, this is still not sufficient, government should conduct regular surveys, increase awareness about the rights and remedies available to women, promote education in remote areas, and should not promote patriarchal mentality as followed in khap panchayats in northern states, etc. At last, I would highlight a quote that, "Overcoming abuse doesn't just happen, it takes positive steps every day. Let today be the day you start to move forward. ~ **ASSUNTA HARRIS.**

CHAPTER ELEVEN

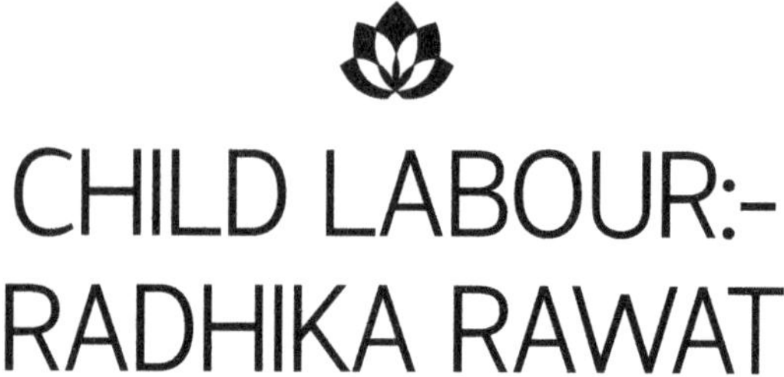

CHILD LABOUR:- RADHIKA RAWAT

BIO- Radhika Rawat is 14 and studying in 10th grade. She is very optimistic and likes peace.
She wants to be an activist so that our world can be a better place to live. She has so many hobbies that she sometimes gets confused about them. Her love for animals is unconditional, enjoys traveling and making new friends. She lives in Delhi.

Child labour refers to the exploitation of children through any form of work that deprives children of their childhood, interferes with their ability to attend regular school, and is mentally, physically, socially, and morally harmful. It is according to Wikipedia but to me, it holds an utterly different meaning it is like plucking blooming flowers and playing with them the way you like. The minute blooming flowers which can become full bloom flowers and become scintillating are all dull after plucking them and garbage after a few hours. The little eyes which should see every amazing thing see slavery and hands slapping them thwacking them, the soft and satiny hands which should be used play in the garden with toys and hold their guardians' hands pick tools in their hand, the ears which should listen to the laughter and pleasant words around them listen to cruel words from their employer. It is like making a child who must feel amity and cordiality pushed into darkness which is tough to escape. Controlling these little lives the way the boss wants.The root cause of this is our mentality. The little blooming flower thinks that earning at an early age without studying is subtle. Parents anticipate this is the only thing their children can do andsupport them financially. The employer thinks they will obey everything and will never revolteven if they have to do back-breaking tasks and will take less money to hire them. Despite that,these are not the most rotten ideologies. It is ours, the people who watch the children working even if we all are educated and know that they do not belong there and conceive that leave it why to bother and be in conflict. It is the mentality of the so-called educated people who are people like me and you. At present children are employed in nearly every working sector and are even involved in unlawful work. Employers make children fear them, and in the time ahead of making these small naive kids like them. Children engaged in all these works are not even a bit productive to the country. The children who ask a lot of questions that cannot even be answered by most educated persons are all wearisome doing the forced work. It is like turning pure gold into faded copper. Around 152 million children are engaged in this terrible field. Child Labour is

a never-ending cycle. The child who is today forced to do labor will also put his child through
this in the future as they encountered it, think labor is the only thing their child can do because
they dont know that these children when bloom completely can change the world and become
successful and touch the skies.Different countries have laid down articles to stop child labor despite these laws it is exercised.We all know child labor is illegal still practiced daily. The only two things that can remove thisfilth from this world are Us and Education. If we support a child and help him from this darkfacade it will motivate everyone to witness this moment that can lead to the complete change of our world.And providing everyone better education can automatically make them think like an alert and good citizen of the country and like a human with a heart, not a greedy and grim
person. When the child who faced child labor reach great heights their parents will regret their
decision to put their gift from God through barbarous work. The kids without parents in this
situation have us all as their family who will defend them from this and support them. This
psyche can change these little lives and this world for good.Use your hands for holding their little hands, your voice for raising it against the callous people who think child labor is ordinary, your mind for changing this poor mindset, andyour heart for love and care for children!

CHAPTER TWELVE

HIDDEN POETRIES OF INCOMPLETE STORIES– HARSH MALHOTRA

BIO:- The "HIDDEN POETRIES OF INCOMPLETE STORIES" written by Harsh Malhotra (Harry), 22 years old. The author is a Web Developer who lives in Delhi, India and he completed his degree in B.Voc (Software Development). His hobbies are to write stories, learning new skills, travelling and listening music. He has a poetry account in Instagram named as @puzzle_ofwords where there are many poetries and stories in Hindi and English.

1. Mystery of Stories:

This Universe is not made up of Atoms
It's made up of Stories
I am a Story. You are a Story.
This Cabbie is a Story
That Tea Seller is a Story too
The Universe is a Story

And all people living in this Universe, they are all Stories.

I'm just trying to capture a few

It is our ability to tell Stories

Stories connect People

Stories combine Love

Some Stories of people we all want to remember because it is inspiring and Valuable to Remember

Some Stories of people we don't want to remember because it's not valuable to remember and it's like Lost Stories in the World

Create your Own Story that others want to Remember and Hear

2. Life is a puzzle between birth and death, it has to be solved by itself

I do not believe that God writes our Destiny

I think we write our own destiny

I believe that God has Written Two Pages of Our Destiny, in which the first page is Birth and the last page is Death.

And In the middle of the book of fate, we have to write pages, which are like a Puzzle,

And we have to solve this Puzzle by writing everything from Challenge, Love, Happiness, Kind, Success, Efforts, and Respects etc.

3. Give your best:

Try your Best to win before the Match is over

Run Run Play Fight Do Everything

You can fight for Live More

You can fight to make your Name to Win to Live in every Match of Life Awaken Your Beast Inside for Completing Challenges

Fire is in your Blood

Once the Match is over, do not think that you Lose or Win

Rather ask yourself, did i give it my very best of it

If your answer is yes then,

YOU ARE WINNER

4. Teachings of Bhagavad-Gita:

It is written in the Bhagavad-Gita,

The problems and crimes of every person,

Are born with his wrong thinking,

And wrong thinking gives wrong idea to the person and this wrong idea often makes the person disturbed and the person often does something in the feelings that he always regrets.

And Shri Krishnan says that wrong thinking can be sanctified and erased,

Only by the nature of love and kindness, so come and speak with me in love Radhe Radhe and be with love and kindness with all

The nature of love and kindness always provides peace and right thinking to a person.

5. Krishna is everywhere:

In Mahabharata, Krishna was everywhere in the army of Korvo and Pandavas Shri Krishna was among those who died in the war

Shri Krishna was also the one who killed the unrighteous.

Who is alive is Krishna

And the dead body is also Shri Krishna.

Every particle of this earth is the abode of Shri Krishna.

Just like Krishna always wins and Krishna always loses

And it goes on till today and will last for eternity

And this cycle of time was rotated by Shri Krishna, which will be a sin only when the pot of sin increases on the earth and this time will not discriminate in any way.

And this cycle has been rotated by Shri Krishna to give better knowledge and better life to the generations to come and reduce sin from the earth.

This time will soon come to an end by Shri Krishna and the time coming after this time will bring better life for the coming generation.

Mahabharata was also composed to bring better happiness life for the coming generation and to reduce sin from the earth.

Keep faith in God

It will soon come to a better life and give the earth a better life.

6. Day of Love:

Someday when you get your love

That night, you will see that your sky is more beautiful than other days You will see that your stars and moon are brighter than other days

You will get all the colours of happiness on that day in your life

On that day, your eyes are brighter than other days

That day, everything you see around you looks pure with your eyes

7. Choose Wisely:

Choose your difficult paths

There may be some passage holes in difficult paths

But the difficult paths always lead to your successful future

There are some tasks in difficult paths that you need to complete for your successful future. Difficult paths build your confidence, attitude and personality

It makes you strong

When you complete the difficult path of your life, you will see yourself where you are standing now

Successful people always choose difficult paths because your efforts to succeed always yield good results.

8. Travellers life:

When Travellers go to Unknown Places, The Life of The Passengers becomes an Adventurous and Joyful Life

When Travellers meet Strangers at Unknown Places, The Memories of Travellers become Great and Memorable

And Some Strangers become a big part of Travellers' lives

And During the Journey, Travellers spend Some Time with Strangers and This Time creates Moments that are Precious Memories

Travellers learn many Lessons of Life through Travel

Sometimes Travellers find The Love of Life from that Place where he/she never been visited before

Travellers start loving some Places while Travellers Travelling

Sometimes Travellers find Happiness and Love from that Place where he/she never been visited before

CHAPTER THIRTEEN

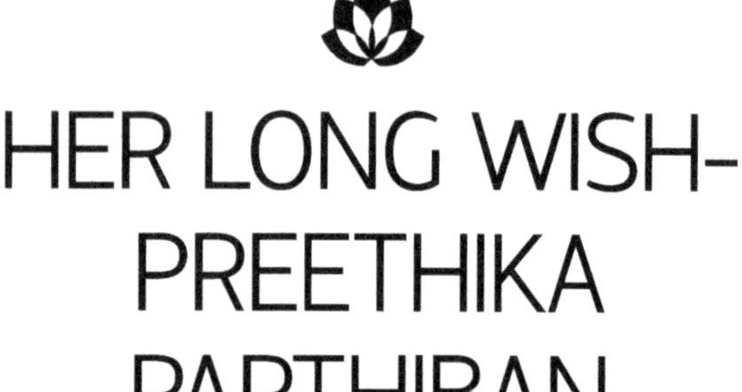

HER LONG WISH- PREETHIKA PARTHIBAN

BIO: Preethika is known for her creativity and logical mind. She is a bibliophile and an aesthetic person. She loves to write her thoughts and blog her reads in her Instagram and website. She is a Master's degree holder in Business Administration.Her longest wish is to become a writer and own her library. One day, if she gets lucky, she will be a member of discovering a time machine.

"Mom, I need to go. It is important please understand.""I am not going to listen to another reason. Now go and change into a traditional dress and greet them.""Mom, I have a meeting right now. It took two months to get the appointment. If we get this business, it will be a milestone. Please understand it is really important to my business.""Are you even listening to me? Bride's family is in our living room. He came from abroad to meet you in person. You are throwing business as a reason to run away again. I am not going to help you this time. Go and change and that's final."I entered my room with a heavy heart. I made a few calls to run the meeting for the next one hour. All I wanted was to close this family drama as soon as possible. I dolled up and came outside. Aarav was there with their family. It was the first-time meeting and he seemed friendly. I sat there for 10 minutes. Everyone's eyes were on me now and then. I wished to disappear like a smoke in the living room. They made me self-conscious about myself. I tried to ignore the awkwardness. I run a café in the center of the city. We are entering a startup fundraiser and it took us months to get into the program. Finally, we were shortlisted by the investors and today we are having meeting with a corporate giant. If we get this funding, we will be able to increase our café revenue to 2X. My fate played again with marriage conspiracy. Like every Indian family, my parents were determined to marry me to the best option this year. This is my 5th awkward meeting with bride family. Every time I doll up and sit in the room as I never exist. No one dare to talk to me as I am bound to be silent. They all back up after they know about my business where they look for a person to stay and take care of their son. Well, why can't they marry a maid who will be there to take care of the household works. This time, its Aarav who came to see me. My mind was fully occupied in the meeting I didn't notice anyone in the room. My father tapped my shoulder and whispered where is my mind right now. Apparently, Aarav was trying to talk and I was in different zone. I apologized and asked Aarav to repeat the question. "So, I heard that you are in business. What kind of a business it is?""Well, it is a café and a coworking space. We have bakery installed and a small restaurant where people can eat and read. It is also included with library so people can work and read in a silent environment. "Nice to hear. Good thought process.""Thank you. How's abroad life and work?""It is good. But I miss my family now and then. They are not coming there as you see. Else it is good there."“Ok."And the silence continued. My parents talked to each other as they know them for a long time. Then Aarav asked if he can talk to me in private.We went to my room. He scanned the room and gave an appreciative nod.“So, you read a lot! Wow, that is a shelf full of awards!"“Well, I am a book worm. Yes, as you see, I sometimes get acknowledgement for the works I do.“I am seeing a different person in this room now. You are a whole package Preethi." “Thank you, Aarav"“How did you get into business by the way?"“My father was in business for some time. He told interesting stories whenever he come home early that time. It motivated me to enter into the business. I love the work and giving something good to the society is something I like about my business."“It is good to know. How much profit are you seeing in the business?"“I have started book café a year ago. Since then, it developed a lot and attracting customers day by day. It is not a lot of profit since it is just a year. It comes around 5 to 6 lakhs per month."“Wow that's great. You know my salary per month is 20 lakhs in US."“That's great to hear."“Preethi, let me get to the point. I like you. I would like to take this to the next level. Since I am moving to US in two months, I want the marriage to happen as soon as possible. Then we have to take visa for you. I wanted to talk in private to know about your opinion."“Hmm. What about my business here!"“You know it is not a serious thing. Sell the business or leave it to someone. US is a dream land and I am earning enough." My nose flared. “So. you are asking me to sell my business? And at what point do you think that it is not serious to you?"“Hey chill, after marriage it is obvious that you have to be with the husband right. What is going to be different?""Tell me Aarav. How will you feel if I ask you to leave your job and come and settle here with me and help me in the business?""Don't be silly. I am getting more income than you. Why I have to leave the job for you?""You answered your question. This conversation is over. This marriage is not happening. You may leave now."He glared and stormed out of the room.I didn't go to see the drama they are making in the living room. I quickly changed to my business casual and arranged my files to leave. My mom entered the room and started to shout. "What is wrong with you? Do you know how big and wealthy their family is? Who gave you the right to talk to the boy like that? I shouldn't have let you educated and I have always opposed the idea. Your father gave you the freedom and look at the way you turned out.""Mom, he didn't care about my business and asked me to leave it just like that. I don't want to marry a person who don't appreciate my interest and value. I am going to the meeting now." I took my car keys and went despite the shout of my mom. I reached my café and went into the conference room. They were discussing about the business proposal we have created. My investors agreed to take the offer. We are now officially promoted to the next level of business establishment. He loved the idea of combining the workspace with a library and restaurant which will attract all types of customers from working professionals to college students. The deal was officially sealed.My friend Ankita came after we finished the meeting."What took you so long? It took me forever to convince them.""You know the family drama and this guy had the gut to step on my ego just because he is earning a lot. I don't have the heart to go to my house now. It is a mess.""Relax Preethi. I will get you something to eat. You are tensed now. Congratulations on our first deal of success." "Thank you Ankita. Without you it wouldn't happen. Let's celebrate it. Gather all our employees, we will have a small inhouse party.:"Yay to the idea Preethi. You are the best!"I smiled and turned the bad mood for some time.I came home by 9:00 PM. It was unusually silent. Maid came and served the dinner. No one was there in sight. "Where is everyone Pattama?""They all went to sleep early madam." "Hmm did they eat dinner?""Yes madam. They had an argument after you left the place. Madam took sleeping pill and BP tablet and went to her room.""Ok. Thank you for helping us today. Go to sleep now."I went to my parent room. They were sleeping peacefully.I sighed and came to my room. I refreshed myself and lied on the bed. I recalled the event happened today.My mother always opposed the idea of me getting educated in the first place. It took me forever to convince them to finish BBA in college. When I asked permission to study MBA, they simply rejected it and asked to study after getting the permission after marriage. I fought my way till this day and started a business. Now I am giving salary to 30 people and helping the orphanage by donating the first half of my profit in the business. My mother rebelled a lot and found this new trend to marry me to the right suitor. It is a puppet show for me. I dress up and sit with them. No one cared about my business and the future I have in mind. Everything was a hurdle for me. Either to convince my parents or to show my self in the public. My achievements were downtrodden because I am a woman. We have evolved a lot with lot of changes. But this gender discrimination is still bugging into people's mind. They don't give much importance to other person's ideas and values. When will this change! When will they understand that women are not only for running a family but more than that? We sacrifice a lot more than we can withstand and still we are not considered as a human being with blood and flesh. When will they understand that some people do like to achieve something in this world? The pressure we put on other gender is impeccable. If a man has to give financial support to the family, a woman needs to nurture and develop the family with all the might she have. What if she doesn't want to start a family? Why it is still considered as a curse when a woman wants to have an independent life! When this will change? I sighed and slept after an hour. I woke up early and went for a jog. My mom was the first one to appear. She came with a big smile. I was surprised. She hugged me and said I am the lucky one."Mom, what is happening?""Aarav's family called now. They accepted this marriage proposal. Aarav is coming to meet you now. Go and get ready.""What is going on? You know what happened yesterday. I am not going to marry that douche bag."Aarav just entered the home and grunted his entry. My mom practically shoved me and welcome him. I was dumbfounded."Hey Preethi" "Hi" !"You must be wondering what is happening now don't you?" "Yes, and with the conversation we had yesterday, I thought it was over.""I understand. I will explain if you forgive me for putting you in a tight spot."I stared at him in disbelief."See, I was not ready for the marriage and my parents were beating themselves to find a better half for myself. I am running an NGO in India in my parent's name and working in US so I that I can help people as much as I can. I wanted a woman with dreams and passion to help the society. When they sent your biodata and photo to me, I was surprised. You are one of the best contributors to Seva Ashram and I know it because I am in their members group. I heard about you a lot and how you are changing the business industry here. That is why I came to India, to meet you in person."I was stupefied and didn't know how to react. He continued."I wanted to check your mindset that is why I put you in a tight spot. I am sorry If I crossed the line. I don't think any one will be the better match for me than you Preethi. As you said, I am leaving US and going to come here and take over my NGO organization and commit my days here to serve the people. I want a woman with passion and love with me to withstand this decision. Will you give me the honor to marry you?"My heart swelled in pride and I said "YES"At last, I saw a human being to share my life with!

CHAPTER FOURTEEN

THE SWEET POTATO KID -ALINA HUSSAIN

BIO: Alina Husain, currently pursuing law, is passionate about writing and speaking up on issues that matter. She tries to depict her truest thoughts in her writings and tries to get emotions into perspective while dealing with the gravity of the issue in hand. Apart from writing, she loves to spend her time reading and exploring multiple ideas and genres. She tries to enjoy her life to the fullest and enjoys bonding with her family and people around her. Music, art and simply watching a good T.V. series or movie are some other sources of rejuvenation for her. She is from New Delhi, India and lives to be an active member of this global society of the present date.

Not long ago did I see a small kid with his carriage on the market road, pulling it and waiting at stops where he could sell people his sweet potatoes. They were December days and I saw him in a single rugged jacket while I saw the others on the road all packed up in all sorts of caps, mufflers and coats. Maybe it was the same poverty that forced this kid to work like an adult, to wear such a non-protective jacket even in such cold days. When I saw him, I felt this strange inquisitiveness inside me which led me to go to his stall and talk to him. I knew that I could not talk to him directly or he would feel strange, for nobody likes to just open up to any stranger and talk about his life. I decided to buy a plate of those sweet potatoes he was selling and started to talk to him. I asked his name and about his residence. He began to answer, pretty much because of a human's basic and intrinsic socialized behavior. As he answered, he said that he has to travel around 10 kilometers every day to just come to the marketplace where he could sell his stuff; in the chilly days, sweet potatoes. As soon as he told me this, I became empathetic since I couldn't imagine a little kid like him to pull that heavy carriage at dawn and dusk for 10 kilometers, every day. He said that he usually starts early around 6 AM and goes back to his home around 10 PM. I knew he couldn't go to school as he works so hard for literally the whole day, but I thought that maybe because of the pandemic, his schooling might have been affected and so, I asked the question. "Do you go to school", I asked, feeling hesitant. "School?", he said, "No", he further added, looking down at the utensil where the sweet potatoes made a cracking noise. "They are ready", he said. "Alright, here's the money", I added.He gave me the paper bowl containing the food and opened a tin lunch box that children use for lunch at school. It contained all the day's hard-earned money and I saw him add the money I gave in his little collection. I ate my food standing near his stall while he patiently waited for the other customers and attended them when required. I finished my food, smiled at that kid and went ahead with the day. Seems disconsolate but not something to be of an extremely problematic nature. Does it? Did nothing extraordinary or problematic occur? Or did we, as a society have failed to understand the situation of that kid? "It's destiny. It's not his mistake that he is born among the poor", they say. Is it destiny? Do we have nothing in our hands as a society that we could do? I want to make myself clear here because I am not saying that we haven't done anything or that we've failed as a democracy to take actions against these cruel situations. I am not saying any of it because I know, we are the world's largest democracy and that in a democracy so large, there are simply going to be people who work towards the better and make true and veritable efforts. All I am trying to say is that there is an inbuilt conscience inside all of us and there's nothing new in it, right? But what's different is that why doesn't it automatically activates itself when we see a little innocent kid selling food or picking up trash or just roaming around looking for one or the other little employment opportunity, she/he could find? Why do we have to think for a moment there to realize that there's something wrong? Why is it so common to see? Why is it not over yet? I could go on forever asking such questions and I feel that if we see a phenomenon so harsh in practice and act like its fate and destiny's play, we have got to keep on asking such questions till the time it no longer exists. Be it years or decades, doesn't matter because what matters is that now we, as a society need to gauge the same problem in an instant, not after taking a few moments to look at the dispirited and disheartened child. We, as a society need to bring this change. I need to. You need to. Everyone else needs to. I know what I am trying here to say is a bit cliché, but it is the true reality. We have got to rise above our present conscious selves and update ourselves to the level where we understand the urgency of the problem, we have in hand. It's not just about feeling sad or expressing the same about such situations. They need our attention now, if we consider ourselves the people who constitute a society, which is today looking forward to develop into its fullest potential. Because no one knows, what the little kid selling those sweet potatoes could become one day. No one. If given the right resources and opportunities and if given a chance to that kid to have real food in his tin lunch box, on a table in a school instead of money in it, on a sweet potato carriage; we cannot even imagine what the children stuck in such muddy puddles like him could bloom and eventually shine into. We don't. If we want to know, we need to just give them all that we can as a society, together.

Thank you so much for taking out the time to read this message.

CHAPTER FIFTEEN

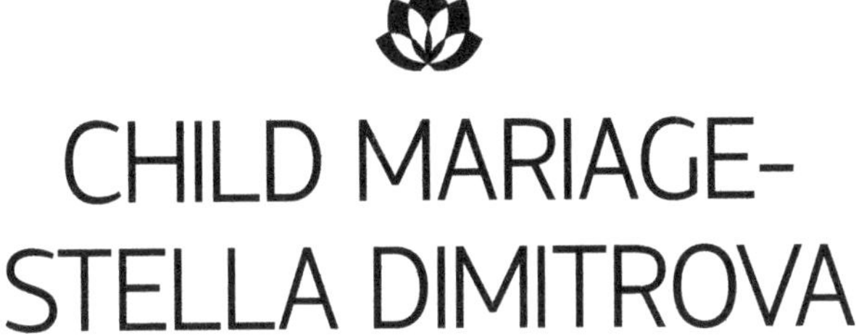

CHILD MARIAGE-STELLA DIMITROVA

BIO:-THE WRITER OF THIS STORY IS STELLA DIMITROVA. STELLA IS A GIRL FILLED WITH JOYFULLNESS, ENTHUSIASM AND AN URGE TO ALWAYS LEARN AND IMPROVE HERSELF. SHE BELONGS FROM BULGARIA.

Today, child marriages are widespread in parts of the world; being most common in South Asia and sub-Saharan Africa, with more than half of the girls in some countries in those regions being married before 18. (I have a right to - BBC World Service) The incidence of child marriage has been falling in most parts of the world. In developed countries child marriage is outlawed or restricted.

In the modern World, generally, parents do not have enough time to spend with their children. Since they do not spend time with their parents, children replace them with technology. The child can read or see something on the internet which can cause harm on his/her psychology since he or she does not know the internet's harmful sides. The difficulty with subsidizing baby attention with administration money is that it fails to give attention to why baby care is so costly from the beginning. Research by the economists Diana Weinert Thomas and Devon Gorry discovered that as such as 20 percent of baby care expenditures would be related to rules that make neither safe nor quality to child care. These rules included this necessity for baby care workers to get high education or college diplomas, which is shown to change well to prices but does not encourage at all to either safety or quality of care. Ruth Lamdan writes: " the many references to baby marriage in the 16th- period Responsa writing and different references, demonstrates that child marriage was indeed common, it was almost the norm. In this context, it is important to mention that at halakha, the term ‘ minor ’ relates to the woman under twelve years and the time. The woman aged twelve and one half was already considered an individual in all respects. " These short term results are undeniable. India's most important cultural barometer, family agency, have already seen falls in " petitions " for grooms settled in the America. One thing is clear, fresh immigrants are getting themselves drawn into the larger public discussion and fight much quicker than they anticipated. Whether immigrants exist here for two generations or two weeks, believing about this larger topic of adoption and " Americanness " by this dominating world constitutes something that will no longer be ignored. We will move in this statement as best we can, yet, one part of us is looking for the question to be answered. Only time can say.

9 798885 914079

Printed by Libri Plureos GmbH in Hamburg,
Germany